10/11

MILITARY VEHICLES

BRADLEY FIGHTING VEHICLES

BY JOHN HAMILTON

VISIT US AT
WWW.ABDOPUBLISHING.COM

Published by ABDO Publishing Company, 8000 West 78th Street, Suite 310, Edina, MN 55439. Copyright ©2012 by Abdo Consulting Group, Inc. International copyrights reserved in all countries. No part of this book may be reproduced in any form without written permission from the publisher. A&D Xtreme™ is a trademark and logo of ABDO Publishing Company.

Printed in the United States of America, North Mankato, Minnesota.
052011
092011

 PRINTED ON RECYCLED PAPER

Editor: Sue Hamilton
Graphic Design: Sue Hamilton
Cover Design: John Hamilton
Cover Photo: U.S. Army
Interior Photos: AP-pgs 21, 28 & 29; Corbis-pgs 6, 7, 18 & 19; Department of Defense-pgs 2, 3, 4, 5, 7 (inset), 10, 11, 12, 13, 14, 15, 16, 17, 20, 22, 23, 24, 25, 26, 27 & 32; Getty Images-pgs 8, 9 & 23 (inset); United States Army-pgs 1, 30 & 31.

Library of Congress Cataloging-in-Publication Data

Hamilton, John, 1959-
  Bradley fighting vehicles / John Hamilton.
      p. cm. -- (Military vehicles)
  Includes index.
  ISBN 978-1-61783-074-7
  1. M2 Bradley infantry fighting vehicle--Juvenile literature. I. Title.
  UG446.5.H283 2011
  623.7'475--dc22
                            2011015972

TABLE OF CONTENTS

BRADLEY FIGHTING VEHICLES

The United States Army's Bradley Fighting Vehicle is an armored, tracked vehicle that transports and protects small groups of soldiers. It is fast, highly maneuverable, and well armed. It can perform multiple missions on the 21st century battlefield.

The Bradley Fighting Vehicle can carry nine people and is designed to be fast. It can go up to 41 miles per hour (66 kph) on a paved road.

The Bradley is an APC, or "armored personnel carrier." But the Bradley is not just a "battle taxi." It supports troops with tremendous firepower, and can even destroy enemy tanks.

Soldiers exit a Bradley to patrol a street in Baghdad, Iraq.

A Bradley's 25mm Bushmaster chain gun is fired at enemy forces in Iraq.

HISTORY

The Bradley Fighting Vehicle was developed in the 1970s as a replacement for the Army's aging M113 armored personnel carrier. The Bradley is faster and better armed than the M113. The first Bradley Fighting Vehicles entered service in 1981.

XTREME FACT The Bradley is named after General Omar Bradley (1893-1981), who commanded American forces during the 1944 D-Day invasion of France in World War II.

BRADLEY VERSIONS

There are two main versions of Bradley Fighting Vehicles. The M2 Infantry Fighting Vehicle version quickly and safely transports a squad of six soldiers to the battlefield and then provides "overwatch" fire to support them.

The M3 Cavalry Fighting Vehicle uses the same chassis as the M2, but its mission is to scout and destroy enemy tanks and other vehicles. It carries only two soldiers in addition to its crew of three. It uses the extra space to haul more missiles and ammunition.

M2 BRADLEY
FAST FACTS

The Bradley is a tracked vehicle, like a tank. It has six road wheels and three track-return rollers on each side.

M2 Bradley Fighting Vehicle Specifications

Length:	21 feet (6.4 m)
Width:	11.8 feet (3.6 m)
Height:	9.8 feet (3 m)
Weight:	33.5 tons (30.4 metric tons)
Top Speed:	41 miles per hour (66 kph)
Cruising Range:	300 miles (483 km)
Crew:	3
Main Weapon:	M242 25mm Bushmaster chain gun
Manufacturer:	BAE Systems
Cost:	$1.54 million (M2A3/M3A3)

CREW

The Bradley has a crew of three: a commander, a gunner, and a driver. The driver sits in the left front of the hull, partially reclining. He sees the battlefield through four periscopes. The commander and gunner sit higher up in the turret.

Driver

One of the Bradley's periscopes may be outfitted with night vision.

XTREME FACT

Gunner

Commander

Up to six soldiers sit in the rear of the vehicle. A hydraulically powered ramp drops down so troops can quickly enter or exit.

ARMOR

The Bradley shields its occupants with layers of aluminum, steel, and laminate armor. The bottom of the hull includes armor to protect against mines. In case the hull is penetrated, the Bradley is equipped with an automatic system that puts out fires.

Bradley armor can stop projectiles as big as 30mm on all four of the vehicle's sides.

A Bradley Fighting Vehicle on patrol in Kuwait. Layers of aluminum, steel, and laminate armor protect the vehicle.

BUSHMASTER CHAIN GUN

The Bradley Fighting Vehicle's main weapon is the M242 25mm Bushmaster chain gun. It can fire armor-piercing or high-explosive ammunition at a range of up to 6,562 feet (2,000 m). The Bushmaster can fire at a normal rate of 200 rounds per minute.

XTREME FACT

The Bushmaster is powerful enough to destroy armored targets, even enemy tanks.

TOW MISSILES

On the left side of the turret, the Bradley is armed with a twin-tubed TOW anti-tank missile launcher. TOW missiles can destroy enemy tanks at a range of almost 2.5 miles (4 km).

Twin-tubed TOW anti-tank missile launcher

*An Iraqi tank explodes after being
hit by a TOW missile shot from a
Bradley Fighting Vehicle in a U.S.
Army demonstration.*

OTHER WEAPONS

In addition to its main weapons, the Bradley Fighting Vehicle is also equipped with an M240C machine gun. Mounted next to the Bushmaster chain gun, the M240C fires 7.62mm rounds of ammunition.

M240C machine gun

For self-protection, the Bradley uses smoke grenade launchers. It can also create smoke with its engine.

ENGINE

Bradley Fighting Vehicles are powered by 600-horsepower, supercharged, 8-cylinder diesel engines. They are designed to be as swift as the Army's M1 Abrams main battle tank, so that they can move in formation together.

AMPHIBIOUS MODE

An M2 Bradley in amphibious mode exits a water obstacle at Fort Benning, Georgia.

Bradley Fighting Vehicles are amphibious, meaning they can operate in water. After a few minutes of preparation, a Bradley can enter the water and move at a maximum speed of about 4.5 miles per hour (7.2 kph), propelled by the motion of its tracks.

COMBAT HISTORY

During the 1990-1991 Persian Gulf War, Bradley Fighting Vehicles destroyed more enemy armored vehicles than even the Army's M1 Abrams tank. Only three Bradleys were lost by enemy fire.

U.S. Army Bradley Fighting Vehicles cross a desert in Saudi Arabia during the Gulf War.

In the War in Iraq, Bradleys were sometimes vulnerable to rocket propelled grenades and explosives hidden

A burning Bradley in Baghdad, Iraq, in 2004.

in roadways. However, casualties were light. The Bradley's effective armor protected the troops inside, who were then able to quickly evacuate.

GLOSSARY

ABRAMS TANK
The Abrams is the United States Army's main battle tank. It is highly mobile and heavily armored. The first M1 Abrams tank entered service in 1980.

AMMUNITION
The bullets and shells used in weapons.

ARMOR
A strong, protective covering made to protect military vehicles.

BATTLE TAXI
A slang term for an armored personnel carrier, such as a Bradley Fighting Vehicle, that protects troops as they are transported to a battle location. Sometimes soldiers shoot from inside the protection of the vehicle until it is safe to dismount.

D-DAY
June 6, 1944. The day during World War II that Allied forces (including the United States, Great Britain, Canada, and other countries) landed on beaches in northern France in order to beat back the forces of Nazi Germany.

DIESEL
A thick petroleum product that is used in diesel engines, such as those found in heavy tanks or trucks.

GRENADE
A bomb with a delayed explosion thrown by hand or shot from a rifle or launcher.

HYDRAULIC
A mechanical system that uses fluids (usually water) under pressure to move heavy objects such as steel doors or ramps.

MANEUVERABLE
Able to change direction and move easily.

OVERWATCH
The tactic of using one military unit, such as a tank, to support and protect another military unit, such as soldiers on the ground.

PERISCOPE
A tubed device made of mirrors that allows a person to see objects outside of an enclosed area.

PERSIAN GULF WAR
A war fought from 1990-1991 in Iraq and Kuwait between the forces of Iraq's President Saddam Hussein and a group of United Nations countries led by the United States.

TURRET
The top part of a tank, which houses the main cannon and other weapons. The turret rotates, allowing a gunner to aim and fire in any direction.

INDEX